Let It Fall

By Maryann Cocca-Leffler

Cartwheel
·B·O·O·K·S·®

SCHOLASTIC INC.

New York   Toronto   London   Auckland   Sydney   Mexico City   New Delhi   Hong Kong

Early mornings,
crisp and cool,

meet new friends
back at school.

Mounds of color,
raked up high—

Jump right in
and watch the sky.

But then...
Chilly, windy, gusty breeze,

rake, rake, rake
the blowing leaves.

our next stop... the County Fair.

Hayrides, contests,

jumping fun.

The winning pumpkin weighs a ton!

But then...
Brother's stroller
piled high,

cold and tired,

say good-bye.

Squirrels gather,
foxes hide,

But soon...
Cold and frosty,
        tall bare trees,

toes and fingers

feel the freeze.

waiting for
our first snowflake.